Why Can't I?

By Melanie Rutherford Ratcliffe

Illustrations by M.C. Sanders

Why Can't I?

Dedication

To my mom — Genice — You are a beautiful example of a godly mother to me and my sisters. Thank you for always putting God first and for loving us so well.

To my incredible children — MaCayla, Leia, and Aiden — Walking this journey with you is one of life's greatest joys. I'm so grateful to have a front-row seat as God shapes your lives, painting each moment with His perfect design. Watching your stories unfold is my greatest blessing. I love you more than words can express.

"Mommy, why can't I?" is how the conversation starts that day, with a pout and a frown as we go out to play.

"Why can't I play with Cayla, who lives down the street? I don't care that she is sick because she is so sweet."

"I know, my love," I say with a smile, "But she doesn't feel well and needs to rest for a while."

"Why can't I?" she whines, her eyes filled with doubt, as she sinks to the floor with her arms stretched out.

"Honey," I say, while smoothing her hair, "There will be other times to play. Don't despair."

Though the setting has changed, the
question remains, whispered now
between ribbons and ballet refrains.

In dance class, I sit, waiting patiently, as my little girl twirls blissfully.

Running and jumping, squealing with delight.
Spinning in circles — a beautiful sight.

Then, all of a sudden, she stands on a chair,
With a giggle and grin, and jumps through the air.

I rush to her quickly to prevent it again. "No more jumping off chairs," I say to her then.

With tears in her eyes and her lip poked out too, she asks in a squeaky voice, "Mommy, why can't I? Liz is doing it too!"

With a gentle voice and knowing glance, I say, "I don't want you to get hurt, so please don't take that chance."

A few months later, sitting on her bed, I read a story while holding her head. We talk and talk into the night about all things important, to my great delight.

She says, "Mommy, why can't I be like you when I get old?"

I laugh and say, "Darling, you can—I am told. What part do you like?"

I ask and then wait. She thinks, then says...

"You get to stay up late,

No homework,

Lots of free time,

And you are nice too!
I want to do that—to be just like you!"

I smile to myself as I turn out the light and think,
Oh man, I must be doing something right!

That was until a few
years later...

Time has passed,

And the statement is rare.
So when I hear it, I can't help but stare.

"Mom, why can't I?" she says with a toss of her hair,
A hand on one hip, and a tone beyond compare.
"All the other girls are going, and I want to go too.
It's not fair! Don't you care? I know what to do."

Gathering my composure, with my temper still in check, I place a hand on her shoulder and say, "You're not grown yet." "Put your phone on my dresser, leave your attitude at the door, I promise, my dear, there's wisdom in store."

"I know you want to go, but I need you to see. I'm keeping you safe. That's what matters to me." "Some lessons take time, and one day you'll know, that love sometimes means saying 'not yet' instead of 'go.'"

"Years ago, you wanted to be like me. Now, what do you think?

Are my values and hopes dropped in a blink?
Do you wish to have someone else around who doesn't care at all?

Or can you take a second to think through this—do you dare to make that call?"

"I love you, my child, more than you will ever know.
What I want for you is the best, and that, in time,
will show.
God is my example of how to live and be,
So, in these difficult times, learn this truth from
me."

A few more years have passed,

And we are packing up her car, to drive away to a college that suddenly seems very far.

"I love you, my dear. You are one of a kind."
I say tearfully, as I hug her tight with my husband standing close behind.

"Mom, thank you for all the love you've given through the years, For every sacrifice and every time you wiped my tears.

You know all my secrets, you've seen me at my worst, Yet you love and care for me—even when it is not deserved.

Your love has been a guide, so steady and so true,

I am forever grateful, Mom, for you."

With a grateful heart, I
tearfully say, "God's love
is what we have and give
to you every day.
Without that, we cannot
do it, so we pray.

Ask Him for help, my dear sweet girl,
and see what He has in store.
You will be amazed to find that it is
more than you could ever ask for."

As she drives off into the world, leaving us behind,
I have a little talk with God and share what's on my
mind.

"Lord, why can't I be there as she takes this giant
step?
I know You hold her in Your hands, but I don't want
her to have regrets."

As I sit on the steps of my now quiet home, I am reminded of a promise that has always been known.

"Do not fear, for I am with you; do not be dismayed, for I am your God. I will strengthen you and help you; I will uphold you with My righteous right hand."
Isaiah 41:10

Lifting my head, I open my eyes, "You are right, my God. I choose faith over fear.
I'll walk forward with Your strength, knowing You are near."

Many years have passed, and now she's full grown,
With a husband, a house, and a child all her own.

As I take out the pie from the oven, still warm,
I hear familiar words that make my heart calm.

"Mommy, why can't I?" her little one says. "Darling,
because I know what is best."

The memories rush back to a time long ago,
Of a diligent mother and a life full of hope.

"God, thank You for this
moment and for my time
on this earth,
To give love to my
daughter and show her
Your worth.

Help her be strong and wise—to know
what to say and do. May her eyes always
be turned to You."

Melanie Rutherford Ratcliffe is passionate about sharing God's love and encouraging others in their faith. With decades of ministry experience, she and her husband, Jody, have devoted their lives to equipping and guiding others in their walk with Christ.

As a wife and mother, Melanie found joy in raising three wonderful children whose lives continue to inspire her storytelling.

She believes in the power of faith-filled stories to nurture young hearts, strengthen trust in God, and encourage mothers to persevere in raising godly children. Through her writing, she hopes to inspire the next generation to walk boldly in faith and embrace God's purpose for their lives.

Margaret (Meg) Sanders is a professor of English, artist, wife, and mother. She believes that everyone has a story worth telling, and enjoys using her art to help bring those stories to life.

Made in the USA
Columbia, SC
07 May 2025

57652283R00020